Teaching Writing:
What the evidence says

UKLA argues for an evidence-informed approach to teaching and testing young children's writing

Henrietta Dombey
with assistance from Myra Barrs, Eve Bearne,
Liz Chamberlain, Teresa Cremin, Susan Ellis,
Prue Goodwin, Andrew Lambirth, Marilyn Mottram,
Debra Myhill, Olivia O'Sullivan, Alayne Öztürk,
David Reedy and Michael Rosen

Contents

Teaching Writing: *What the evidence says*

Introduction: what success has to teach us

In England our schools are more closely regulated than ever before. A detailed National Curriculum combined with a regime of inspection (with punitive sanctions) aimed at ensuring methodological conformity is intended to raise Standards. To many people not immediately engaged with the classroom, the way to do this seems obvious. Focus heavily on the basics, such as spelling and punctuation. Apply rigour, in the form of grammar teaching. Test frequently. But if we look at the research evidence, as we will see, the answers are rather different.

Writing is about constructing and encoding meaning. It is therefore a more complex and demanding process than reading and consequently harder to learn. One researcher claims that engaging in a writing task is as mentally demanding as playing chess. (Kellogg, 2008). Eliot is not alone in his experience of "the intolerable wrestle with words and meanings" (Eliot, 1941, part II lines 20-21).

There are a number of primary schools in the UK and elsewhere where children enjoy writing, do so with ease and verve, and score well on tests. Yet many other children are not enthusiastic and writing scores on England's SAT tests have been consistently lower than scores for reading. If we are to improve national standards in writing, we need to learn from the success stories. This booklet aims to help readers to do this.

The research cited here comes from the English-speaking world, primarily from the UK, the US, Australia and New Zealand. Some of our knowledge comes from intervention studies, some from surveys (including Ofsted surveys) and some from observational studies. In recent years, studies of teacher and school effectiveness have made an important contribution, and so we devote a substantial section of this paper to insights from this work. We recognise the value of all these research paradigms as sources of information about how children go about the business of writing, how they can best be helped to learn to write – and to become writers, exploiting the rich possibilities that written text has to offer for enlarging their lives.

2   What writing is and how we go about it

2.1 What writing involves

If we are to teach our children to write most effectively, we need to be fully aware of what writing is and what it can do. The act of writing is about constructing what the writer wants to say, in a visual form, using the communicative tools and practices available (Kress, 1997). So learning to write is more than the mastery of the range of technical skills and transcriptional conventions that determine how words should be set down on the page or screen. Composition - the construction of meaning through words - is central. We should emphasise at this point that the evidence on the teaching that works best suggests that learning to write is most effectively achieved through approaches that balance communicative purpose and technical skills (Knapp *et al.*, 1995; Medwell *et al.*, 1998; Louden *et al.*, 2005).

In almost any piece of writing, from a substantial novel to a note on the kitchen table, a writer has to bring together:

- a sense of what has to be communicated - a purpose for writing;

- a knowledge of who might read the text and how to speak to them without the support of a shared context - a sense of audience;

- a familiarity with the explicit language of written text and its lexical, grammatical and presentational forms;

- an awareness of different types of writing, both paper-based and digital, and which might best fit the purpose and audience;

- a knowledge of punctuation and spelling;

- control of handwriting or digital technology;

- a readiness to review the writing after the first draft, checking for sense, for fitness for purpose and audience, and for technical accuracy.

Cremin and Myhill (2011) state that writing requires us to:

Shape our thoughts into words, frame those words into sentences and texts which are appropriate for our intended audience and purpose, and pay attention to shaping letters, spelling words, punctuating sentences and organizing the whole text. (Cremin and Myhill, 2011, p.10)

2.2 What writing can do

However, writing is not just one, undifferentiated kind of activity: different purposes require different kinds of writing.

The writer can use writing to:

- record events, through log books, diaries etc.;
- work out ideas and shape emerging thoughts, through jottings, drawings and notes and wikis;
- order and extend thinking, as in planning for action or developing an argument;
- reflect on experiences, ideas or learning, through journals, logs and diaries;
- create aesthetically satisfying works, such as stories, poems and plays;
- communicate with others, both known and unknown, in a range of formal and informal ways, through texting, e-mails, letters, work reports etc.

These purposes are not all mutually exclusive: some writing may be for the writer alone, but most writing has a communicative function, an audience in mind. In addition, engaging in the act of writing builds a cultural identity for the writer, an authorial persona. To write is to extend one's relationship with the world and one's role in it.

2.3 The changing nature of text

Writing these days is not just about words alone: in the world outside school the nature of texts has changed dramatically in the last few decades. Advances in digital technology have opened out possibilities, allowing texts to have a much stronger visual component with the added possibility of sound and video. Electronic texts of all sorts can be copied, modified and forwarded in ways that make them much less static than conventional texts and blur the boundaries between reading and writing. Today, text composition is as much about design as it is about verbal choice (Bearne, 2005; Kress, 2008).

2.4 Going about a piece of writing

So how do we go about this complex task? Over 30 years ago, Hayes and Flower (1980) proposed that the experienced writer engages in three different kinds of activity: planning, creating text and reviewing. In their view, this is not a simple three-stage sequence, but a process in which the writer weaves back and forth between all three activities in the course of writing a single text.

For children learning to write, any piece of writing involves, of course, a further kind of activity, in that spelling, punctuation and handwriting - skills that experienced writers use almost automatically - require conscious attention, at least in the early years of primary school. So to become independent writers, children have to learn to orchestrate many different kinds of skill, knowledge and understanding, bringing them into harmony to create a satisfying and effective text.

The different functions of writing listed above have an importance for children learning to write as well as for experienced writers. Writing as an instrument for shaping thought has a particular significance. Building on the work of Hayes and Flower cited above, Bereiter and Scardamalia (1982), see that to become effective writers, children not only have to learn to write for known and unknown readers, they also need to move from 'knowledge-telling' to 'knowledge-transforming'. In short, children need to learn to exploit the opportunity offered by writing to develop their thinking and understanding, through using the act of writing to order, explore, extend, clarify and revise their view of the world and their place in it. This concern is now widely shared: Neuman and Roskos (1997) argue that children need to learn not only the technical skills of reading and writing but also how to use these tools to develop their thinking and reasoning.

In addition, we need to be aware that teaching children to write is a social and cultural act. Cremin and Myhill (2011) write:

> *When we write we are participating in a social practice that is shaped by social and historical understandings of what writing is and what texts should do. When we teach children to write, we teach them what is valued in our culture.* (Cremin and Myhill, 2011, p. 11)

What follows is based on this view of writing as a cognitive, social and cultural act, focused on the making of meaning, much more than the sum of its technical parts.

3 Children becoming writers: what they bring to school

So what do we know of how children best learn this complex skill, form of expression, way of thinking, way of being in the world?

Learning to write doesn't just happen in school. Children come to school with a range of competences, experiences, attitudes and expectations that affect what they make of what school has to offer. The last few decades have established beyond contradiction the importance of this early learning. We look in turn at the spoken language children bring to school, their experience of hearing stories read aloud and their familiarity with nursery rhymes and word play, as well as their experience of writing letters and their names.

3.1 Spoken language

Here longitudinal studies have been informative. The work of Gordon Wells (1985) and Garton and Pratt (1989), in particular, show that children whose pre-school language develops most substantially are at an advantage in learning to write and do so more effectively. To learn to write is easier for children who have a secure grasp of spoken language and an awareness of what it can do (Clay, 1998). This should not surprise us as learning to write is about making meaning through language and the more substantial a child's experience of spoken language, the greater the resources available for making meanings in this new way and the greater their awareness of the power of language.

3.2 Experience of hearing written text read aloud

But experience of hearing written texts read aloud offers something more. England's *Bookstart* project (http://www.bookstart.org.uk/), now 20 years old, has helped to spread this highly productive practice more widely. A meta-analysis by Bus *et al.* (1995) of studies of pre-school book-sharing at home shows joint book reading by parents and pre-schoolers to be significantly related to a range of outcome measures such as language growth and emergent literacy.

Case studies show that listening to stories gives children not only a wider vocabulary (Hepburn *et al.*, 2010), but also a wider repertoire of syntactic structures, a sense of the shape of a whole text, and a growing awareness of the range of meanings stories have to offer (Dombey, 1994). In particular,

Fox's pioneering study of pre-school children's story-telling demonstrates powerfully how children can put this knowledge to productive use in shaping and articulating their own narratives (Fox, 1993). In listening to engaging stories read aloud in ways that invite involvement, children are not only beginning to experience some of the pleasures of the written word, they are also becoming familiar with its contours, its tropes and the resources it offers for the construction of meaning.

3.3 Nursery rhymes and word play

Nursery rhymes encapsulate the pleasure young children find in language play. Their patterned language communicates a shape and order that is belied by the dramatically nonsensical, knockabout content. They draw attention to the sounds of language, helping children bring to conscious awareness the initial consonant sounds ('onsets') and the back part ('rimes') of such words as 'wall' and 'fall', 'wool' and 'full'. Bradley and Bryant (1983) have shown such word play to be positively associated with subsequent success in learning to read and write.

Goswami and Bryant (1990) point to the power and importance of young children's capacity to build analogies, which they see as accounting for the clear connection between pre-school awareness of rhyme and alliteration and later progress in reading and spelling. Maclean, *et al.* (1987) found that three-year-old children's knowledge of nursery rhymes specifically related to their more abstract phonological knowledge later on. In the preschool years, sensitizing children to sound similarities does not seem to best achieved through formal training but rather comes from listening to patterned, predictable texts while enjoying the sound and meanings that the language produces (Neuman and Roskos, 1997).

3.4 Early attempts at writing

There is evidence that children under three can recognise the differences between writing and drawing (Karmiloff-Smith, 1992). But although many young children engage in mark-making, this cannot be classed as either writing or drawing, since it has features of both: through their marks these very young children are exploring the principles underlying the symbolic systems of both drawing and writing (Lancaster, 2007).

With experience, children come to differentiate the two forms of representation. Over time, children's experiments with writing move closer to the models in their environment. More than two decades ago, Ferreiro and Teberosky (1982) showed how through such experimentation, young children in Mexico City's slums developed increasingly apt theories about how writing works.

Nearly all pre-school children have some sense of the purposes of written language - of its importance in commercial transactions and in the personal lives of those around them (Solsken, 1993). Many of them have been involved in writing shopping lists, greeting cards and letters. Increasing numbers will also have experience of using a computer keyboard, through play on an adult computer or on a keyboard toy of their own.

Children who arrive at school already able to write their names without copying from a model are likely to make better progress in aspects of learning to write than children not yet able to do this (Blatchford, 1991). Similarly children who arrive with a knowledge of letters of the alphabet are at an advantage (Riley, 1996). But, bizarrely, Riley has also shown that teaching children to recognise these in a pre-school setting does not appear to confer advantage in literacy learning (Riley, 1996). It seems that the ability to write one's name and recognise letters of the alphabet is a symptom of a close acquaintance with reading and writing used in purposeful and enjoyable ways and that it is the anchoring of this technical know-how in this deeper knowledge that prepares children for school literacy learning.

Early attempts at writing can help children acquire a working knowledge of the alphabetic system. A classic study by Read (1971) found that even without formal spelling instruction, preschoolers use their tacit knowledge of phonological relations to spell words. Citing findings by Bissex (1980) and Teale and Sulzby (1986), Neuman and Roskos (1997) sum up the embedded nature of the most productive pre-school learning in this area when they state:

Children's earliest discoveries about written language are learned through active engagement with their social and cultural worlds. (Neuman and Roskos, 1997, p. 10).

Experience of digital texts seems to operate in a very similar way: children learn through using the new technologies in interaction with others and for purposes that make sense to them (Yamada-Rice, 2010; Levy, 2011).

4 Children becoming writers: what they have to learn in school

All children arrive in the Reception class with knowledge and experience that is relevant to learning to write. But this knowledge and experience is likely to differ widely in kind and extent. Many children may have 'had a go' at writing, in play or in cards to family members, or on the computer, some may also have listened to over a thousand stories read aloud, some may have engaged in shared story-telling and some may have memorised songs. Many children with a home language other than English may have 'had a go' at writing in a script based on different principles from those of English orthography. All these different kinds of learning need to be recognised, valued and continued.

So too do children's out-of-school experiences of digital writing, which are likely to increase as children get older. A 21st Century curriculum needs to reflect the increasingly multimodal forms of writing children engage with (Bearne and Wolstencroft, 2007; Cremin and Myhill, 2011). If the definition of writing is broadened to reflect such practices as digital games, texts messages and web-design, many children say they write for pleasure (Lenhart et al, 2008, Clark and Dugdale, 2009). There is also some evidence to suggest that young people who have their own social networking page have more positive attitudes towards writing (Clark & Dugdale, 2009).

Of course these out-of-school experiences of writing are not enough: children need to learn to use the written word to create, with increasing independence and technical accuracy, an increasing range of meanings for an increasing range of purposes and audiences as they make their way up the primary school. However, those who say they enjoy writing and those who write outside of school are more likely to be writing above the level expected for their age (Clark, 2012).

As to the process of writing, ultimately children need to learn to think up and note down ideas about what they are going to say, turn those ideas into the actuality of words - with images and sounds in some cases - that speak to an unknown reader in a comprehensible and coherent way. They also need to learn to set the words down on the page or screen without conscious attention to how they are spelled or how the letters are formed, review what they have written, refining it to make it communicate more effectively and do all this in a recursive way, moving between amending their plans, forging new text and polishing what they have produced.

We should stress again that what we know of what works best (see sections 5 and 6) suggests that learning to write in this broad sense is most effectively achieved through approaches that balance communicative purpose and technical skills (Knapp *et al.*, 1995; Medwell *et al.*, 1998; Louden *et al.*, 2005).

Certainly sustained, explicit instruction in technical features, removed from the context of purposeful use, does not seem to be the most effective way to teach these lessons. So what is set out below is most definitely not a teaching or learning sequence.

In school, children need to learn to:

4.1 Experience what writing can do

Children need a felt experience of the range of purposes writing serves, from notes to jog the memory to personal messages, sets of instructions, stories, poems and explanations. They need to learn how writing weaves through and has the potential to shape a range of experiences and social relationships. They need to understand how writing can capture, organise and transcend experience, and how it marks and shapes their daily lives.

4.2 Produce the language of written text

Even those children with a good grasp of spoken language, a familiarity with using words to get things done, to recount past events and plan the future, still have to learn written language. Some start to do this at home in the pre-school years; others need to learn this in school. Unless they learn what written language is like and what it can do, learning to write in school is likely to be a baffling and largely meaningless task.

Written language differs from spoken language in both its form and its function. It is, of course, more permanent than talk. In addition, unlike spoken language, it usually has to be understood in a different context from the context of its production, so it has to be more explicit. Intonation, facial expression, bodily stance, gesture and shared physical surroundings are all useful supports for spoken language, helping conversational partners understand each other. But, apart from presentations supported by digital technology, written texts usually have to stand on their own. So the choice of words, their arrangement and punctuation – together with the text's design, font, size and colour – have to bear a heavy communicative weight.

Other than the informal language of tweets and text messages, written language tends to use denser structures - expanded noun phrases rather than simple ones, sentences rather than loosely connected clause complexes, and cohesive stretches of text with thematic unity rather than the meanders of conversation. So learning to write is learning to produce written language as well as learning to put the words down on the page.

Standard English is predominantly the dialect of written language. This can add another layer of difficulty for children who use another variety of English at home, and provides a further argument for ensuring that all children are thoroughly engaged with reading and listening to written language in the classroom.

4.3 Develop a personal voice

While children need to learn the language of written text, they should also be helped to develop their own voices, express their own ways of seeing the world - and operating in it. Through written text, particularly expressive or poetic text, children should be able to communicate who they are and what matters to them in a manner that takes into account the audience and purpose of the piece.

4.4 Shape writing to meet its various purposes

The study of genre has been much stressed in recent years; it remains important to initiate children into mastering the cultural expectations for different kinds of writing. This is partly to do with the way the subject matter is conceptualised for different purposes, partly the shape and pattern of different genres and partly the relationship set up with the reader through indicators of formality or informality.

4.5 Exploit the potential of written language

Children need to learn to use written language to explore and develop new ideas. This requires an emphasis on the way in which written language allows the writer to examine what they think, exploring its inconsistencies and implications. It makes a virtue of the plasticity of writing - the potential it has for amendment and re-shaping. Insistence on a neat and complete first draft is likely to hinder this process.

4.6 Construct multimodal text

Combining written language with other modes of representation prepares children to operate in today's world. This involves the non-linear presentation of verbal and iconic text (words and pictures), using the tools of design, such as variations in layout, font size, shape and colour, on paper and screen, with awareness of how each mode contributes to the meaning (see Bearne *et al.*. 2004). This, it must be emphasised, is an essential part of learning to write in the 21st century.

4.7 Develop a fluent handwriting style

In our electronic world, a fluent handwriting style is still important. Children who write more easily tend to write better texts (Medwell and Wray, 2007). The ability to write without conscious attention to letter formation allows children to focus on the content of what they write, freeing up working memory to deal with the complex tasks of composition and revision. Automatic letter writing appears to be the single best predictor of length and quality of written composition in the primary years (Graham, *et al.*, 1997).

So the development of a legible, easy, fluent handwriting matters. To say this is not to advocate a dominant concern with the appearance of children's written work: over-attention to neatness may be counter-productive. Nor, as suggested above, is it to recommend specific attention to handwriting out of the context of message construction.

But mastering the letters of the alphabet is not a trivial matter. As Gorman and Brooks (1996) have shown, learning to write alphabet letters correctly involves careful observation, good hand control and hand-eye co-ordination. More recent studies have shown that handwriting is far from a simply motor act: it is "language by hand" (Berninger and Graham, 1998) in which orthographic and memory processes make a bigger contribution than motor skills (Berninger and Amtmann, 2004).

4.8 Develop keyboard skills

Keyboard skills are not learned automatically and need to be provided for if children are to word process effectively. Explicit keyboarding instruction (touch-typing) is necessary if the full potential of the word processor is to be unlocked for children's writing (Connelly et al. 2010). But as with handwriting, such instruction needs to be balanced with attention to meaning.

4.9 Become confident and accurate spellers

English spelling is notoriously difficult, reflecting the long and complex history of written English. The majority of words in English are not phonetically 'transparent' as in many other languages, such as Spanish. Whereas context clues may provide useful information for the identification of problem words in reading, there is no equivalent source of help in spelling.

Children in primary school therefore need to acquire a wide range of spelling knowledge:

phonological awareness, which includes, as well as awareness of individual phonemes, attention to syllables, onsets and rimes;

letter names and alphabetic knowledge, since a ready familiarity with letters is indispensible for learning to write English;

a growing lexicon of known words, which is particularly important in English as very many of the commonest words, such as ''one' and 'two' do not follow any straightforward rules;

visual awareness of the likely patterns that occur in English spelling, so that they can tell whether a word they have written 'looks right';

awareness of common strings and patterns, such as 'igh' and 'ittle';

a growing knowledge of word structures and meanings, including prefixes, suffixes, compound words, word roots and families and word origins.

Gentry (1982) identified children's developing mastery of the orthography of English as a 5 phase process in which early use of random letters is followed by phases in which children attend, increasingly closely, to the phonemes of the words they wish to write, finally turning to visual patterns, as they enter what Gentry terms the 'Conventional' phase, which is marked by correct spelling. This, of course, takes many years to achieve for English spellings and progress is not even. Indeed, any piece of writing by a child rarely represents one single phase.

Through analysis of case studies, more recent work has confirmed that Gentry's phases are not discrete, as most children draw on a variety of different kinds of knowledge from the beginning, although for each child, one strategy - phonetic or visual - tends to dominate (O'Sullivan and Thomas, 2007). It should be noted that children should focus on correct spelling when texts are being revised, rather than during the composition process, when the choice of words must be the prime concern (Knapp *et al.*, 1995).

4.10 Punctuate effectively

Punctuation seems less important to young writers than getting the words down on the page. When they do begin to use punctuation marks, they tend to distribute them across and around their writing in ways that appear random or based on visual appearance. As Nigel Hall states, "Children need to move from [these] graphic principles, which are a dead end, to the use of linguistic principles which open up the world of punctuation." (Hall, 2001, p. 147). They need to learn to use question marks and exclamation marks to show the status of what is written, and tell the reader how to speak it. They need to use commas, full stops and capital letters to indicate units of meaning.

4.11 Write in English, whatever their home language

Children who come from homes where English is not dominant (or perhaps not even present) have more to learn than their monolingual classmates. But evidence suggests that where their home language competencies are respected and good provision is made for learning English, they are likely to do almost as well in English as monolingual children, as they reach the top of the primary school. At the end of Key Stage 2 in 2011, 72 per cent of EAL and bilingual pupils achieved the expected level in both English and mathematics at the end of Key Stage 2 compared to 75 per cent of pupils whose first language is English (NALDIC, 2012). This means that the difference narrowed by 4 points, from the 7 point difference in 2007 (NALDIC, 2012).

Bilingual children also have the social and cognitive advantages that come from experiencing different ways of conceptualizing the world (Baker, 2006) While the challenge of engaging with all the learning outlined above in a second (or third) language adds a layer of complexity to the early stages of learning to write, research has shown that bilingual and multilingual children are not confused by this process (Gregory, 1996; Kenner, 2004; Robertson, 2004). However, in the early stages at least, they may need particular support in the compositional aspects of learning to write.

4.12 In summary

Learning to write is not a straightforwardly technical matter. It is a multi-stranded process, that involves social as well as cognitive learning and that contributes to the development of children as thinkers who have a sense of their identities, their possibilities and their relations with others. The texts produced may be multimodal, involving drawings, photographs, video and/or sound clips. But many of their written texts have to be able stand on their own, distant in time and space from their authors. As they are produced, all these varieties of written texts have the potential to build new meaning for their authors.

A proper balance between the meaning-related and technical aspects of learning to write is essential. As Warrington *et al.* (2006) put it:

> *Teaching writing means more than instruction in technicalities: it means providing a balance between helping young writers develop a personal voice and ensuring that they also know how to present well-structured and accurately written texts.* (Warrington *et al.*, 2006, p. 145)

Developing a personal voice is not a cosmetic matter: it is about using writing to express and shape the individual's view of self, others and the events, phenomena and meanings of the wider world. When children learn to write they are "learning to represent their world", and therefore, in order to shape the text, children need "to draw on their personal interpretations of the world and events" (Christie, 2003, p. 288).

We need to encourage and support children's attempts to make personal meaning from school-based writing practices and ensure that they are active participants in their own learning **(Cremin & Myhill, 2011; Lankshear and Knobel, 2003).**

5   Lessons from studies of effective schools and effective classrooms

We have much to learn from research over the last few decades about how children with varying experiences and expectations of written language can best be helped to learn all that it takes to become a writer. We look first at the many studies of what characterises learning and teaching in classrooms and schools where the teaching of writing has been seen to be most effective, then at the many classroom practices that have proved productive.

Kathy Hall (2013) has recently reviewed the evidence from anglophone countries concerning effective teaching of literacy in the early years of school. Citing numerous studies over the last two decades, she concludes that "effective literacy teaching in the early years of school is about far more than method. Rather it is a complex mix of philosophy, method, teacher development and school culture." (Hall, 2013, p. 535).

Effective literacy teachers:

5.1 Balance the technical and compositional aspects of learning to write

Detailed observational and interview studies of exemplary teachers carried out in the US by Pressley *et al.* (1996), Block and Pressley (2000) and by Pressley *et al.* (2001) show that these highly effective teachers offer children a wide range of reading and writing experiences, including daily writing in journals and writing workshops as well as mini-lessons about the mechanics of writing, based on children's needs. In kindergarten (but not at grade 1 or 2) this often involves repeating these literacy experiences, using the same text and context until the child makes the connection. At all three grade levels, in any single lesson, the exceptional teachers do not focus on one or two teaching points, but teach up to twenty different skills in a single hour. The evidence of Wilkinson and Townsend (2000) from four outstanding early years teachers in New Zealand is broadly in line with these findings.

5.2 Integrate these aspects of learning to write

Balance is important, but balance is far from all in the classrooms of effective teachers. Attention to technical features is contextualized in the process of purposeful writing. In a study of effective teachers of children in the first six grades in New York City, Knapp *et al.* (1995) observed that they teach skills as tools to be used immediately, not items to be learned for their own sake. This is borne out by the findings about effective teachers of literacy throughout the primary age-range by Medwell *et al.* (1998) in England, Wilkinson and Townsend (2000) in New Zealand and Louden *et al.* (2005) in Australia.

5.3 Emphasise attention, engagement, metalinguistics and challenge

Effective teachers are distinguished from their less successful colleagues not only by the activities they engage in, nor simply by making clear and obviously relevant to the children the purpose of any technical features under discussion. In their study of early years classes in Australia, Louden *et al.* (2005) found that the more effective teachers go about their activities in a particular way: they place greater emphasis on attention and engagement, metalanguage and challenge.

5.4 Give priority to a richly conceived literacy

In New Zealand, Parr and Limbrick (2010) looked at the teaching of writing throughout the primary years, in schools achieving high results in an area that was normally low-achieving. They found that literacy is a clear priority for teachers in the most effective schools and noted that pupils both read more and write more on topics they care about than their age-mates do in less effective schools. In the US, Knapp *et al.* (1995) found that effective teachers make creativity and self-expression important in their classrooms. Children in both studies spend more time on task, apparently enjoying what they do. In England, Medwell *et al.* (1998) found a similar focus.

5.5 Spend more time in small group teaching

The Center for the Improvement of Early Reading Achievement (CIERA), a US government-funded research initiative, has carried out a number of studies including a national study of effective schools in high-poverty inner-city areas (e.g. Taylor *et al.*, 1999; Taylor *et al.*, 2000). They find that such schools are organized to maximize the possibility of small group work. The composition of these groups is seen to be important, with groups that are based on similar levels of attainment, but are not static, instead changing frequently in the light of continuous assessment and monitoring. Lower-achieving groups are not confined to mundane tasks. Focusing on the teaching of writing, Parr and Limbrick (2010) make a similar observation, showing that their effective teachers spend more time in small group teaching than is the norm, again making careful use of assessment and monitoring to adjust the composition of the groups. However, they also note "Effective practice is not something absolute; it varies with context." (Parr and Limbrick, 2010, p.586).

5.6 Know what their pupils can do and what they need

Medwell et al. (1998) note that effective teachers are also marked out by their use of focused observation, systematic record-keeping and skilful use of more and different support for struggling writers. Such features also mark the classrooms of the effective schools in the CIERA studies (e.g. Taylor *et al.*, 1999; Taylor *et al.*, 2000).

5.7 Create more discursive, conversational and dialogic classrooms

Classrooms where children achieve greater success in their literacy learning are certainly orderly places, where teaching is explicit and expectations are clearly transmitted to children. But the order is democratic rather than autocratic: the shaping of written text takes place within a general atmosphere of tentativeness, negotiation and dialogue (Taylor *et al.*, 1999; Taylor *et al.*., 2000; Knapp *et al.*, 1995).

5.8 Build explicitly on children's personal and cultural backgrounds

The teachers in Parr and Limbrick's (2010) study demonstrate knowledge of the children's out-of-school lives, and reflect this knowledge in the print environment of the classroom and in the kinds of writing the children are asked to engage in. The work of the classroom is not culturally separated from the children's homes, but recognises, values and builds on their home experiences.

5.9 Share the purposes for writing and the criteria of success with learners

Studies show not only that effective teachers are marked by the clarity of their explanations, but also that they offer timely and focused feedback and that all this is within the context of a sense of purpose shared with the children (Knapp *et al.*, 1995; Taylor *et al.*, 1999; Taylor *et al.*, 2000; Louden *et al.*, 2010; Parr and Limbrick, 2010).

The actions of effective literacy teachers are founded on beliefs - about literacy, teaching and children - that set them apart them from their less successful colleagues.

The practice of the most effective teachers is supported by their philosophies (Medwell *et al.*, 1998; Parr and Limbrick, 2010). These teachers have a stronger focus on meaning and place more importance on children's recognition of the purpose and function of particular literacy activities; they also see all pupils as capable of becoming effective writers (Wharton-McDonald *et al*, 1998; Block and Pressley, 2000; Taylor *et al.*, 2000; Block et al., 2002; Au *et al*, 2005; Parr and Limbrick, 2010). The most effective teachers see their pupils as active, thinking, feeling sense-makers and apply their theoretical understanding not just to the class in general, but to particular children.

Such approaches, dispositions and beliefs appear to be more important than curricular content.

6 Key classroom practices that promote development in writing

The previous section itemised findings from successful schools and classrooms. This section is mainly concerned with studies of innovative practices introduced into classrooms, with beneficial results.

One message that comes through very many of the research studies cited in the previous section is that if children are to be fully engaged in their learning they need to experience learning to write as interesting, meaningful and purposeful from the start, which means that they should not be confined to exercises in letter formation in the early stages, but involved in purposeful activities such as shared story-writing and the exchange of written messages. We need to ensure that classrooms are responsive to the knowledge, skills and concerns that children bring to school and supportive to the generation of ideas that take the children into new territory. What follows is a list of practices aimed to do just this.

Children tend to make a good start in learning to write where their teachers:

6.1 Model and share the process of writing

But how can children start to produce meaningful texts while also getting to grips with the technical aspects of writing? Children need to learn to combine a complex array of skilled activities into one coherent (if not always smooth) operation. Re-enthusing teachers in the writing process can be an excellent starting point. Visiting children's authors who talk about how they go about writing can provide a way in (Cremin *et al.*, 2010).

Modelling writing involves the teacher in constructing a composition in front of the class, on a large surface, 'thinking out loud' as she goes, thus demonstrating the many kinds of choices involved in composition. The topic is chosen to engage the children's interest. Through this activity, the teacher can draw attention to writing as a process of orchestrating knowledge and skills, and show how to maintain a focus on the subject matter, and a sense of the purpose and audience for the text, while also dealing with necessary technical matters. This is often achieved through a sequence of some or all of the processes of informal and formal planning, drafting, revising, proof-reading and preparing the text for publication. (Fisher, 2002).

Even more effective is the practice of Shared writing, where the children are actively involved in both choosing the words and setting them down on the paper. This has been shown to be highly effective, (Laycock, 2011) particularly where the writing is directed at meeting a purpose recognized by the children as important. The teacher's management of the processes of composition, transcription and revision provides a framework in which many different aspects of the process can be experienced and brought together, leading to a recognisably accomplished outcome. Perhaps the most important feature is the discussion through which the text is composed and revised. This offers the possibility of developing meta-linguistic awareness, of exploring how different words arrangements and punctuation marks construct different meanings.

This approach can be particularly constructive for children in Reception and Year 1, learning to set words down on paper for the first time, as Geekie *et al.* (1999) show most powerfully in their study of a highly effective Reception Class teacher. The children start each day by helping their teacher scribe a one-sentence 'story' about a shared experience. At other points in the day the children show, in their attempts to record their own stories, how much they have learned from this shared experience. In both contexts, as she listens and talks to the children, the teacher's aim is to help them achieve what they cannot yet do on their own.

6.2 Invite the exchange of written messages

The postbox in the corner of the classroom at Key Stage 1 is one way to make writing a matter of real communication for young children. So too can be the teacher's response to a child's story or account of an experience. There is the world of difference between "good try" and "I got lost too, when I was your age." The danger that writing becomes an empty exercise to please the teacher is always present: exchanging purposeful messages can re-engage children in the process (Block and Pressley, 2000).

Electronic communication can make the act of writing particularly engaging. By Year 2 children can be enthusiastically and productively involved in texting, message boards, Twitter and sites such as Club Penguin (Waller, 2010; Marsh, 2012). In these contexts writing becomes fun for many more young learners, who come to see the point of careful composition and transcription.

6.3 Encourage the use of talk in the writing process

Latham (2002) has shown that talk can extend the capacity of working memory for writing - a particularly important consideration where young novices are concerned. In a Scottish study, children in Reception wrote significantly better when they talked through the writing process with a Year 6 child who had struggled in the early years of learning to write (Nixon and Topping, 2001). Talk between children seems to facilitate the internalisation of processes demonstrated by the teacher and can assist children in deciding what to say and how to spell (Davidson, 2007).

6.4 Support invented spelling

English orthography is notoriously complex. We should not expect children to get it right from the start. Research shows that children use a variety of useful spelling strategies from the early stages - phonetic, visual and known words.

In the early phases of learning to spell, the most productive approaches to helping children make progress appear to be support, encouragement and purposeful writing (Bissex, 1980): children learn to spell through trying to do so as they write and should be encouraged to monitor their own spellings from early on, with support from teacher and peers.

Encouraging invented spellings in these early stages helps children get their own words down on the page. But to progress, visual approaches - 'remembering how words look' - are necessary as well as 'sounding words out'. Explicit teaching makes the biggest difference in moving children towards conventional spelling (Peters, 1970).

More recent work has not challenged these findings. Instead it has reinforced the idea that to learn to spell effectively in English, children need to be trained to attend to both the sounds of words, their visual configurations and, as spelling develops, the structure of words (suffixes, prefixes, word roots etc) (O'Sullivan and Thomas, 2007).

6.5 Encourage play with rhyme and alliteration

Young children enter enthusiastically into play with the sound of language. The academic pay-off is that they become more aware of speech as sequences of phonemes and so better prepared to learn phonics and spell. Sharing nursery rhymes and tongue twisters brings the added benefit of showing the enjoyable nonsense that can be created through language. The research studies of Bryant *et al.* (1989), Goswami (1999) and Coyne *et al.* (2012) have shown a clear connection between experience and knowledge of rhyme and alliteration and later progress in reading and spelling.

Children continue to make progress where their teachers:

6.6 Engage in writing themselves, sharing experience and expertise with their classes

McKinney and Georgis (2009) and Yeo (2007) have shown that teachers' childhood experiences of writing in school have an impact on their identities as writers and teachers of writing. Not all those experiences were positive or transfer well into today's classrooms. Gannon and Davies (2007) show that many teachers are drawn to teach English by a love of reading but are less enthusiastic about writing and often lack assurance as writers. When teachers develop such an assurance however, this can, scholars argue, have a positive effect on their teaching (Andrews, 2008; Ofsted, 2009). Studies by Pritchard (1987) Cremin (2006) and Cremin and Baker (2010) suggest that when teachers readily engage in writing themselves, they come to reconsider and transform their pedagogic practice and may show increased empathy for younger writers.

6.7 Work with children, demonstrating the process of writing, acting as scribes, response partners, editors and advisors

Vygotsky's (1978) conception of effective learning, produced as a novice shares a task with a more experienced practitioner, and Bruner's notion of scaffolding are often loosely invoked to justify a variety of teaching approaches (Wood, Bruner and Ross, 1976). By contrast, the work of Cremin and Baker identifies a series of contexts in which teachers share the writing task with their students productively to scaffold their learning. They show the effectiveness of teachers taking a range of supporting roles, helping children develop confidence and competence as young writers (Cremin, 2006; Cremin and Baker, 2010). The teachers may be involved as:

> authentic demonstrators in front of the whole class, showing how they go about such varied task elements as choosing a topic, selecting the write words, revising the word order and remembering spellings;

> scribes for whole class joint compositions, where children have the support of both the teacher and each other as they jointly construct a shared text;

writers alongside the children in small group contexts, where they can create a genuine 'workshop' atmosphere as both teacher and children wrestle with the choice of words and the task of setting them down;

response partners, helping children to become aware of how others see their writing;

editors and advisers, perhaps closer to the more traditional teacher role, but here aimed towards offering authorial advice and helping children make wise choices as writers, rather than correcting their writing;

publishers, enabling children to present their writing to a wider audience.

6.8 Encourage and support wide and copious reading

When published authors give advice about becoming writers they invariably tell their audience to read as much as possible. Ofsted's survey of 12 outstanding schools revealed that visits to libraries, plentiful reading aloud by teachers and the provision of good-quality up-to-date texts stimulated pupils to read more and inspired them with ideas for their own writing (Ofsted, 2011). Children who read more write more and write better.

Since the 1980s, research evidence has shown that reading and being read to help children to develop models for writing: children who read particular genres, such as stories using metafictive devices, can be inspired to create something of their own in that genre, in which, for example, the narrator directly addresses the reader (Pantaleo, 2007b). Stories they have read may also suggest events or predicaments for children to include in their own texts. Indeed for children as well as adults, all writing is intertextual. As Cairney writes:

Each new text written reflects, in some measure, the shadows of texts experienced in the past. (Cairney, 1990, p.484)

Arguably the most pervasive effect appears to be on the texture of the young writers' written language: on the vocabulary, sentence structure and cohesive patterning through which they create complex webs of meaning (Cairney, 1990; Sipe, 1993; Frater, 2001; Pantaleo, 2007a).

6.9 Regularly read substantial texts aloud

Studies carried out in the 1960s showed that listening to stories read aloud in engaging ways at school has a significant effect on children's vocabulary (Fodor, 1966; Cohen, 1968). Elley (1989) also shows that reading aloud to

7 and 8 year olds in school provides them with a significant source of vocabulary expansion. But the effect goes wider than vocabulary. In an experimental study of reading aloud to kindergarten and first grade children, Vivas (1996) shows, as well as improved vocabulary and story comprehension, increases in the range of syntactic structures and the width of linguistic activity in the classroom.

This is richly demonstrated in the report of a research project carried by staff at the Centre for Language in Primary Education with Year 5 teachers in schools in South and East London (Barrs and Cork, 2001). Working with rhythmic and resonant texts, some of them common to all five classes, the six teachers strove to engage children through animated reading aloud, dramatisation and related activities, including discussion of key features of the texts.

Over the year of the project, dramatic changes in the children's writing became evident. In all classrooms the literary text had become a source and an inspiration for writing. But how the text was used varied across the classrooms. The teacher's activities most positively associated with improved scores and to writing of high quality were reading and re-reading aloud, intervening and responding to children's texts during the process of writing, and reading their work aloud to them.

6.10 Make links between reading and writing

A recent descriptive study of interactive read-alouds in writers' workshop sessions in a third grade class (Manak, 2011) shows explicit discussion led by the class teacher playing an apparently key role in enabling children to make connections between the texts they read and hear, and those they write. As well as reading aloud, the teacher explained the purpose of particular features of the text and also made explicit connections between the students' reading and writing experiences. Making such connections also encourages children to think of themselves as writers and of writing as a way of exploring the world and their relation to it (Smith, 1982; Calkins, 1994).

6.11 Make extensive use of drama, involving children in writing arising out of this

Children are particularly responsive to drama - to the idea of taking on other roles, imaginatively living other's lives, investigating fictional scenarios and exploring the implications of their actions through their multimodal engagement. Such engagement invites children to 'inhabit' a text, giving it a new urgency, and prompting an exploratory yet focused use of language. Drama has an important role to play in literacy education. Primary phase research indicates that it has a positive effect on learners' achievements in writing, producing more depth and detail (Barrs and Cork, 2001; Crumpler and Schneider, 2002; Fleming *et al.*, 2004; Cremin *et al.*, 2006). In particular, when teachers 'seize the moment' for children to write during drama, the tense scenarios of the imagined experience offer a supportive scaffold that fosters thoughtful, imaginative and effective writing (Cremin *et al.*, 2006).

6.12 Encourage language play

Research into children's language play indicates that children's delight in playing with rhyme, rhythm and tune contributes to their learning of the sounds, structures and meanings of language and to its symbolic use (Opie, 1993; Grugeon, 1999). Drawing on children's enthusiasm for playing with language, their spontaneous use of rhythm, rhyme, alliteration and assonance enriches their writing of poetry (Cummings, 2007). Their poetical experiences may best be nurtured by building bridges between their existing knowledge of language play and the new knowledge of poetry encountered in the classroom.

6.13 Foster choice and independence in writing

Schools that are hospitable to their students' out-of-school lives, including the writing practices of their homes and communities, evoke a greater commitment to learning to write and a greater sense of the importance of writing (Nixon and Comber, 2006). Other research into connections between home and school indicates that fostering choice and enabling connections to be made between writing at home and at school can increase motivation, commitment and quality (Rowe and Neitzel, 2010). Close studies of what children actually write have shown that the topics and the materials they choose to engage with emerge from their social and cultural experiences and the practices in their homes and communities (Walsh, 2007).

6.14 Provide authentic purposes for writing and allow children to choose their own topics

Unsurprisingly, children appear to write better when writing on topics that matter to them (Teale and Gambrell, 2007). Some students know what they want to write about, whether this is about an area of expertise or an adventure story. Others may be at a loss and need a context and a purpose to commit themselves to. The teacher may create the context, perhaps a drama involving many different roles and perspectives on events, but if the students are given choices about the forms, perspectives, audiences and purposes of their writing, they are more likely to be engaged and committed (Cunningham and Allington, 1999; Cremin *et al.*, 2006; Walsh, 2007; Bearne *et al.*, 2011).

Writing journals, which usually take the form of books in which children are free to write (and also draw) on topics of their own choosing, provide a valuable context in which children from the Foundation Stage to Year 6 are free to explore their own particular concerns. Used carefully, as described by Graham and Johnson (2012), they can have a markedly positive effect on children's attitudes and attainment in this area. It is important that the teacher treats the journal as the child's property and an indicator of his or her interests and thinking. So the teacher's role is not to correct transcription errors, but, where invited to do so, to respond to the substance of what the child has written.

6.15 Find time for children to write every day and also to engage in sustained periods of writing

Like all complex skills, writing is not easily or quickly mastered. It needs practice. Of course this does not mean mechanical drills and empty exercises. It means daily and sustained engagement with writing that is playful, purposeful, fed by rich experiences of drama, poetry and story as well as explanatory and descriptive texts. But the time devoted to writing is crucial. Evidence from successful classrooms in the US and England demonstrates the need both for daily writing and for sustained periods of writing (longer as the children get older) in which children produce substantial texts (Cunningham and Allington, 1999; Berninger *et al.*, 2006; Ofsted, 2011).

6.16 Encourage the use of talk as an aid to writing

The work of Mercer and Littleton has demonstrated conclusively the power of disciplined, purposeful small group talk to promote children's learning across the curriculum (Mercer and Littleton, 2007). Drawing on Vygotsky's conception of learning as most powerful when it is collaborative (Vygotsky, 1978), they have shown, in primary phase classrooms, that focused talk can enable children to use language to think and learn together, to organize ideas and to solve problems. This has huge implications for the teaching of writing.

Corden (2000) demonstrates the enhanced writing that follows from the careful fostering of talk in both group and whole class contexts. Building on Corden's work, Fisher *et al.* (2010) have focused on the use of talk in response pairs to generate idea, as oral rehearsal (or 'writing aloud') and as reflection about the process of writing. Others have also seen the value of such reflective talk, both on the process of writing and on the sense of what it is to be a writer (Cremin, 2006; Feigenbaum, 2010). In particular, working with response partners appears to prompt young writers to become readers of their own texts and thus helps develop the inner voice of a critically reflective writer (Yarrow and Topping, 2001; Feigenbaum, 2010).

The creative experience of oral storytelling of old and new tales has also been shown to make a rich contribution to children's narrative writing and to their creative capacity to transform texts (Grainger, 2001).

6.17 Establish writing workshops

Donald Graves (1983), who initiated the shift in focus from writing as product to writing as process, maintained that there are four essential elements to a successful writing-process program: the adequate provision of time (at least 4 sessions per week), child choice of writing topic, response to child meaning, and the establishment of a community of learners - a community that has learned to help itself. The *Writing Workshop* approach aims to treat children as writers who have areas of expertise and interesting ideas to communicate.

The approach involves interaction between children and with the teacher at various stages of the process: brainstorming, topic selection, drafting, revision, editing and publication. While there appears to be limited research on the quantifiable effects of introducing this approach, it is likely to be productive, since it embodies very many of the features that, as shown above, have proved successful in raising the quality of writing in the primary years. In addition, the Ofsted report *Excellence in English* (Ofsted, 2011), which presents the practice of twelve exemplary schools, includes a focus on the writing workshop approach adopted by one primary school, with dramatically positive effect.

Children make progress where their teachers also teach those crucial technical lessons...

6.18 Spelling

Encouraging invented spellings in the early stages helps children get their own words down on the page (Treiman, 1994). But to progress, a wider range of strategies including visual approaches is necessary, as well as 'sounding words out' (Snowling, 1993). In particular, work on misspellings (Dix, 2006), and the collection of similarly spelled words have been shown to be productive, as has attention to word meanings (Hilte and Reitsma, 2011).

Effective teaching has been shown to operate through such activities as: 'mini lessons', classroom word collections, displays and print hunts focused on different aspects of spelling, grouping of content or 'topic words', words with common meanings, similar letter strings and patterns, words with the same prefix, or suffix etc. (O'Sullivan and Thomas, 2007).

6.19 Handwriting and keyboard skills

Word processing offers unparalleled opportunities for the revision, exchange and presentation of text. It should not be reserved for the publication of children's texts, but should also be used for their composition. However, if these opportunities are to be fully exploited, children need to be at ease with the keyboard, not tapping out their texts laboriously, one letter at a time. Explicit keyboarding instruction (touch-typing) is necessary if the full potential of the word processor is to be unlocked for children's writing (Connelly *et al.*, 2010).

Yet a fluent handwriting style is still important. Recent studies have shown that children who write more easily tend to write better texts (Berninger and Amtmann, 2004; Medwell and Wray, 2007). This is not simply a matter of training the fine muscles of the hand: handwriting not a simply motor act, but can more usefully be thought of as "language by hand" in which orthographic and memory processes make a bigger contribution than motor skills (Berninger and Graham, 1998). As with other technical aspects of the writing process, handwriting and keyboard skills are best learned in the context of producing meaningful text.

6.20 Punctuation

Calkins (1980) found that in classrooms where writing was purposeful and attention was focused on the effect on the reader, 8 to 9-year-olds used a wider variety of marks and did so more effectively than their age mates in classrooms where writing was more regulated and punctuation learned by rules. Hall's research (2001) with 5 and 6-year-olds tells a similar story. He found that meaningful understanding of punctuation results from a combination of the following: meaningful reading and writing activities, talk about punctuation emphasising the effect it produces, encouragement of an experimental approach, a well punctuated classroom environment. An important contribution was also made by the teacher's self-discipline in limiting herself to one type of explanation for punctuation - either elocutionary (how the text should be read aloud), grammatical (how punctuation indicates syntactic divisions and relationships) or semantic (how it shows meaning). Skill in using punctuation is also supported by children's experience of a range of text forms, and a classroom ethos in which talk about learning is ongoing and interest in punctuation marks is encouraged.

However, the children Hall observed to make most progress in their use of punctuation were given very little explanation by the teacher. The principal criterion they used in deciding on whether to use a particular mark was semantic - what the mark would make the words mean.

6.21 Grammar teaching

Robust research evidence about the direct relationship between teaching primary children knowledge about language or grammar and any beneficial impact on their writing remains very limited. Two significant large-scale meta-analyses of studies nearly all carried out with secondary students, (Hillocks, 1986; Andrews *et al.*, 2006) found no evidence of a relationship. It should be noted that these studies concern the teaching of grammar separated from the teaching of writing.

However, more recent projects have involved teaching grammar in the context of writing. Working with children aged 6 to 10 in Scotland, Hunt (2001) has shown that introducing key terms such as 'synonym' 'verb', 'noun', 'sentence' and 'noun phrase' in the context of shared writing can clarify the options and so help children consider alternative wordings and make appropriate choices. Meanwhile in Australia, Williams (1995) has explored how aspects of the meaning-oriented model of systemic linguistics can be grasped by 6 to 11-year olds. Any effect on their writing has not been documented.

Recently in England, a study by Myhill *et al.* (2012) involving a large-scale randomised trial in secondary schools found significant positive effects for teaching that included explicit attention to relevant grammatical constructions within the context of writing. But the authors note that not all pupils benefited equally, finding "a more marked positive effect on able writers" (Myhill *et al.* 2012 p.151).

This study was carried out in secondary schools, where a sustained meta-linguistic focus might be considered more developmentally appropriate, than in primary school, not least because many of the technical processes of writing have already been mastered by most children before entry to secondary education. But, as indicated above, the teaching of writing inevitably involves the use of some meta-linguistic terms. We do not yet know which of these terms are likely to be most productive in the primary years, at which stage, or how they might best be introduced.

7 Assessment

To have value in informing decisions about the paths to be taken by students or teachers, any system of assessment needs take account of the more important aspects of writing outlined above. As the evidence cited makes clear, learning to write involves learning to compose written language, suitable to the purpose served by the writing and the audience at which it is directed. It is much more than spelling, punctuation, handwriting and the appropriate use of grammatical structures.

It is essential that any assessment of writing reflect this fact. Assessment for the purposes of monitoring, for audiences within the school or beyond it, must also recognise the complex nature of learning to write. Selecting aspects of transcription to stand proxy for the whole complex process will not yield useful results. Especially where such information is used to judge schools and teachers, it will instead lead to an over-emphasis on one part of learning to write at the expense of other vital aspects.

8 Conclusion

As this survey of a wide range of research findings has repeatedly shown, it is not useful to divorce technical matters, whether grammatical or secretarial, from the business of learning to compose written text for a range of audiences and purposes. Starting off with activities as modest as a message to a friend, popped into the classroom postbox, children need to know that writing is about communication and ideas.

In classrooms where young children learn to write effectively, attention is given to both the learning of the codes of written language and also to the uses and purposes of writing, in ways that are meaningful to the learner. Teachers provide extensive opportunities for their pupils to read and respond to children's literature and to write for a variety of authentic purposes while also attending to the codes of written language - to grammar, sound-symbol correspondence, spelling patterns, punctuation, and text structure. Ironically, while they need explicit teaching, these more mechanical skills appear to be best learned in the context of engagement with powerful literature and writing a range of texts for purposes and audiences that matter to the writer.

In these successful twenty-first century classrooms there is no longer a sharp divide between the written word and other modes of communication. Today children come to school with experiences and expectations of multimodal text. When they leave school it is to make their way in a world dominated by proliferating digital forms of communication. We owe it to our children not to try to recreate the classrooms of sixty years ago, but to allow them to benefit from the rich lessons research has given us over the intervening decades about how children learn to write and what the new technologies have to offer. In this way we can help them take possession of the written word and use it to make sense of their lives, and the world around them. Teaching children to write is too important for us not to do it as richly as we can.

References

Andrews, R.C. (2008) *Getting Going: Generating, shaping and developing ideas in writing*. London: Department for Children, Schools and Families.

Andrews, R.C., Torgerson, S., Beverton, A., Freeman, T., Lock, G., Low, G., Robinson, A. & Zhu, D. (2006) The effect of grammar teaching on writing development. *British Education Research Journal* 32, 1, pp. 39-55.

Au, K. (2005) Negotiating the slippery slope: school change and literacy achievement. *Journal Of Literacy Research* 37, 3, Pp. 267-286.

Baker, C. (2006) *Foundations of Bilingual Education and Bilingualism*. 4th edn. Clevedon: Multilingual Matters.

Barrs, M. & Cork, V. (2001) *The Reader in the Writer: The links between the study of literature and writing development at key Stage 2*. London: Centre for Language in Primary Education.

Bearne, E. (2005) *Making Progress in Writing*. London: Routledge.

Bearne, E., Chamberlain, L., Cremin, T. And Mottram, M. (2011) *Teaching Writing Effectively: Reviewing practice*. Leicester: United Kingdom Literacy Association.

Bearne, E., Ellis, S., Graham, L., Hulme, P., Meiner, J. & Wolstencroft, H. (2005) *More than Words 2: Creating stories on page and screen*. London: Qualifications and Curriculum Authority, Royston: United Kingdom Literacy Association.

Bearne, E., Ellis, S., Graham, L., Hulme, P., Merchant, G. And Mills, C. (2004) *More than Words: Multimodal Texts in the Classroom*. London: Qualifications and Curriculum Authority, Royston: United Kingdom Literacy Association.

Bearne, E. & Wolstencroft, H. (2005) Playing with possibilities: children and computer texts. In J. Marsh and E. Millard (eds.) *Popular Literacies, Childhood and Schooling*. London: RoutledgeFalmer.

Bearne, E. & Wolstencroft, H. (2007) *Visual Approaches to Teaching Writing: Multimodal literacy 5 - 11*. London: Sage with UKLA.

Bereiter, C. & Scardamalia, M. (1982) 'From conversation to composition: the role of instruction in a developmental process.' In R. Glaser (ed.)

Advances in Instructional Psychology. Vol 2. Hillsdale NJ: Lawrence Erlbaum Associates pp. 1-64.

Berninger, V.W. & Amtmann, D. (2004) Preventing written expression disabilities through early and continuing assessment and intervention for handwriting and/or spelling problems. In L. Swanson, K. Harris and S. Graham (eds.) *Handbook of Research on Learning Disabilities.* New York: Guilford Press pp. 345-363.

Berninger, V.W. & Graham, S. (1998) language by hand: a synthesis of a decade of research on handwriting. *Handwriting Review* 12, pp 11-25.

Berninger, V.W., Rutberg, J., Abbot, R., Garcia, N., Anderson-Youngstrom, M., Brooks, A. & Fulton, C. (2006) Tier 1 and tier 2 early intervention for handwriting and composing. *Journal of School Psychology*, 44, 1, pp. 3-30.

Bissex, G. (1980) *GNYS AT WRK: A child learns to write and read.* Cambridge MA: Harvard University Press.

Blatchford, P. (1991) 'Children's handwriting at 7 years: associations with handwriting on school entry and pre-school factors', *British Journal of Educational Psychology* 61, 1, pp. 73-84.

Block, C.C., Oakar, M. And Hurt, N. (2002) The expertise of literacy teachers: a continuum from preschool to grade 5. *Reading Research Quarterly* 37, 2, 178-206.

Block, C.C. And Pressley, M. (2000) It's not scripted lessons but challenging and personalized interactions that distinguish effective from less effective primary classrooms. Paper presented at the National Reading Conference Phoenix, December.

Bradley, L. And Bryant, P. (1983) Categorising sounds and learning to read: a causal connection. *Nature*, 301, 419-421.

Bryant, P. E.,Maclean, M., Bradley, L. & Crossland, J. (1989) Nursery Rhymes, Phonological Skills and Reading. *Journal of Child Language* 16, pp. 406-428.

Bus, A.G., Ijzendoorn, M.H. And Pellegrini, A.D. (1995) Joint book reading makes for success in learning to read: a meta-analysis on intergenerational transmission of literacy. *Review of Educational Research*, 65, 1, 1-21.

Cairney, T. (1990) Intertextuality: infectious echoes from the past. *The Reading Teacher* 43, 7, pp. 478-484.

Calkins, L. (1980) When children want to punctuate: basic skills belong in context. Language Arts 57, pp. 567-573. 1994) *The Art of Teaching Writing.* Portsmouth N.H.: Heinemann.

Christie, F. (2003) 'Writing the World'. in N. Hall, J. Larson and J. Marsh (eds.), *Handbook of Early Childhood Literacy*. London: Sage.

Clark, C. (2012) *Young People's Writing in 2011: Findings from the National Literacy Trust's annual literacy survey*. London: National Literacy Trust.

Clark, C. & Dugdale, G. (2009) *Young People's Writing: Attitudes, behaviour and the role of technology*. London: National Literacy Trust.

Clay, M.M. (1998) *By Different Paths to Common Outcomes*. York, Maine: Stenhouse.

Cohen, D. (1968) The effect of literature on vocabulary and reading achievement. *Elementary English* 45, 2, pp. 209-213.

Connelly, V., Gee, D. & Walsh, E. (2010) A comparison of keyboarded and handwritten compositions and the relationship with transcription speed. *British Journal of Educational Psychology*, 77, pp. 479-492.

Corden, R. (2000) *Literacy and Learning through Talk*. Buckingham: Open University Press.

Coyne, E., Farrington-Flint, L., Underwood, J. & Stiller, J. (2012) Sensitivity to rime unit frequency and children's early word-reading strategies. *Journal of Research in Reading* 35, 4, pp. 393-410.

Cremin, T. (2006) Creativity, uncertainty and discomfort: teachers as writers. *Cambridge Journal of Education* 36, 3, pp. 415-433.

Cremin, T & Baker, S (2010). Exploring teacher-writer identities in the classroom: conceptualising the struggle. *English Teaching: Practice and Critique*, 9, 3, pp. 8-25.

Cremin, T., Goouch, K., Blakemore, L., Goff, E. & Macdonald, R. (2006). Connecting drama and writing: seizing the moment to write. *Research In Drama in Education*, 11(3), pp. 273-291.

Cremin, T. & Myhill, D. (2011) *Writing Voices: Creating communities of writers*. London: Routledge.

Cremin, T., Reedy, D., Sprackland, J. & Starling, I. (2010) *Writers in Schools*. (CD Rom) Leicester: United Kingdom Literacy Association.

Crumpler, T. & Schneider, J. (2002) Writing with their whole being: a cross study analysis of children's writing from five classrooms using process drama. *Research in Drama Education* 7, pp. 61-79.

Cummings, R. (2007) Language play in the classroom: encouraging children's intuitive creativity with words through poetry. *Literacy* 41, 2, pp. 93-101.

Cunningham, P.M. & Allington, R.L. (1999). *Classrooms that Work: They can all read and write*. New York: Longman.

Davidson, C. (2007). Independent writing in current approaches to writing instruction: What have we overlooked? *English Teaching: Practice and Critique*, 6, 1, pp. 11-24.

Dix, S. (2006), "What did I change and why did I do it?" Young writers' revision practices. *Literacy*, 40, 1, pp. 3-10.

Dombey, H. (1994) Narrative in the nursery class. International *Journal of Early Years Education*, 2, 3, pp. 38-53.

Eliot, T.S. (1941) *East Coker* from *Four Quartets*. London: Faber and Faber.

Elley W. B. (1989). Vocabulary acquisition from listening to stories. *Reading Research Quarterly*, 24, pp. 174-187.

Feigenbaum, F. (2010) Development of communicative competence through private and inner speech. In A. Winsler, C. Fernyhough and I. Montero (eds), *Private speech, Executive Functioning, and the Development of Verbal Self-Regulation*. pp. 102-20 Cambridge: Cambridge University Press.

Ferreiro, E & Teberosky, A. (1982) *Literacy before Schooling*. Portsmouth NH: Heinemann.

Fisher, R. (2002) Shared thinking: metacognitive modelling in the literacy hour. *Reading* 36,2, pp. 63-67.

Fisher, R, Myhill, D., Jones, S. & Larkin, S. (2010) *Using Talk to Support Writing*. London: Sage.

Fleming, M., Merrell, C. & Tymms, P. (2004) The impact of drama on pupils' language, mathematics and attitude in two primary schools. *Research in Drama Education* 8, 2, pp. 221-230.

Fodor, E. (1966) *The Effect of the Systematic Reading of Stories on the Language Development of Culturally Deprived Children*. PhD thesis Cornell University.

Fox, C. (1993) *At the Very Edge of the Forest: The influence of literature on story-telling by children*. London: Cassell.

Frater, G. (2001) *Effective Practice in Writing at Key Stage 2*. London: The Basic Skills Agency.

Gannon, G. & Davies, C. (2007) For the love of the word: English teaching, affect and writing. *Changing English*, 14, 1, pp. 87-98.

Garton, A. & Pratt, C. (1989) *Learning to be Literate: The development of written and spoken language* (2nd edn.). Oxford: Blackwell.

Geekie, P., Cambourne, B. & Fitzsimmons, P. (1999) *Understanding Literacy Development*. Stoke on Trent: Trentham Books.

Gentry, J. (1982) An Analysis of Developmental Spelling in GNYS AT WRK. *The Reading Teacher* 36, pp. 192-200.

Gorman, T. & Brooks, G. (1996) *Assessing Young Children's Writing*. London: Basic Skills Agency.

Goswami, U. (1999) Causal connections in beginning reading: the importance of rhyme. *Journal of Research in Reading* 22, 3, pp. 217-240.

Goswami, U. & Bryant, P (1990) *Phonological Skills and Learning to Read*. Hillsdale NJ: Lawrence Erlbaum.

Graham, L. & Johnson, A. (2012) *Children's Writing Journals*. (Rev. edn.) Leicester: United Kingdom Literacy Association.

Graham, S., Berninger, V., Abbot, R., Abbott, S. & Whittaker, D. (1997) The role of mechanics in composing of elementary school students: a new methodological approach. *Journal of Educational Psychology,* 89, 1, pp. 170-182.

Grainger, T. (2001) Crick Crack Chin, My Story's in: Stories and Storytelling, in P. Goodwin (ed.) *The Articulate Classroom*. London: David Fulton.

Graves, D. (1983) *Writing: Teachers and children at work*. Portsmouth N.H.: Heinemann.

Gregory, E (1996) *Making Sense of a New World: Learning to read in a second language. London: Paul Chapman.*

Grugeon, E. (1999) The state of play: children's oral culture literacy and learning. *Reading* April pp.13-16.

Hall, K. (2013) Effective literacy teaching in the early years of school: a review of the evidence. In J. Larson and J.Marsh (eds.) *The Sage Handbook of Early Childhood Literacy*. Rev. edn. London: Sage pp. 523-540.

Hall, N. (2001) Developing understanding of punctuation with young readers and writers. In J. Evans (ed.) *The Writing Classroom: Aspects of writing and the primary child 3-11*. London David Fulton.

Hayes, J. & Flower, L. (1980) Identifying the organization of writing processes in L.Gregg and E. Steinberg (eds.) *Cognitive Processes in Writing*. Hillsdale NJ: Lawrence Erlbaum Associates pp. 3-30.

Hepburn, E., Egan, B. & Flynn, N. (2010) Vocabulary acquisition in young children: the role of the story. *Journal of Early Childhood Literacy*. 10, 2, pp. 159-182.

Hillocks, G. (1986) *Research on Written Composition: New directions for teaching*. Urbana IL: National of Teachers of English.

Hilte, M. & Reitsma, P. (2011) Activating the meaning of a word facilitates the integration of orthography: evidence from spelling exercises in beginning spellers. *Journal of Research in Reading* 34, 3, pp. 333-345.

Hunt, G. (2001) Raising awareness of grammar through shared writing. In J. Evans (ed.) *The Writing Classroom: Aspects of writing and the primary child 3-11*. London David Fulton.

Karmiloff-Smith, A. (1992) *Beyond Modularity: A developmental perspective on cognitive science*. Cambridge MA: MIT Press.

Kellogg, R. (2008) Training writing skills: A cognitive developmental perspective. *Journal of Writing Research*, 1, pp. 1-26.

Kenner, C. (2004) *Becoming Biliterate: Children learning different writing systems*. Stoke on Trent: Trentham Books.

Knapp, M.S. and Associates (1995) *Teaching for Meaning in High-Poverty Classrooms*. New York: Teachers' College Press.

Kress, G.R. (1997) *Before Writing: Re-thinking the paths to literacy*. London: Routledge.

Kress, G.R. (2008) *Reading Images: Multimodality, representation and new media*. www.knowledgepresentation.org/BuildingTheFuture/Kress2/Kress2

Lancaster, L. (2007) Representing the ways of the world: how children under three start to use syntax in graphic signs. *Journal of Early Childhood Literacy* 7,2, pp. 123-152.

Lankshear, C. & Knobel, M. (2003) *New Literacies: Changing knowledge and classroom learning*. Buckingham: Open University Press.

Latham, D. (2002) *How Children Learn To Write: Supporting and developing children's writing in schools*. London: Paul Chapman.

Laycock, L. (2011) Shared Reading and Shared Writing at Key Stage 1. In P. Goodwin (ed.) (3rd ed.) *The Literate Classroom*. London: David Fulton.

Lenhart, A., Arafeh, S., Smith, A. & Rankin Macgill, A. (2008) *Writing, Technology and Teens*, Pew Internet.

Levy, R. (2011) Young children, digital technology and interaction with text. In M. Thomas, (ed.) *Deconstructing Digital Natives: Young people, technology and the new literacies*, New York: Routledge.

Louden, W., Rohl, M., Barrat-Pugh, C., Brown, C., Cairney, T., Elderfield, J., House, H., Meiers, M., Rivaland, J., & Rowe, K.J. (2005). In teachers' hands: effective literacy teaching practices in the early years of schooling. *Australian Journal of Language and Literacy*, 28, 3, pp. 173-252 (Whole issue).

Maclean, M. Bryant, P. E. & Bradley, L. (1987) Rhymes, nursery rhymes and reading in childhood. *Merrill-Palmer Quarterly*, 33, pp. 255-282.

Manak, J. (2011) The social construction of intertextuality and literary understanding: the impact of interactive read-alouds on the writing of third grade writers during writing workshop. *Reading Research Quarterly*, 46,4, pp. 309-311.

Marsh, J. (2012) Purposes for literacy in children's use of the online world 'Club Penguin'. *Journal of Research in Reading* first published online 11 June 2012 in advance of print publication.

McKinney, M. & Giorgis, C. (2009). Narrating and performing identity: Literacy specialists' writing identities. *Journal of Literacy Research*, 41, 1, pp. 104-149.

Medwell, J., Wray, D, Poulson, L. & Fox, R. (1998) *Effective Teachers of Literacy*. Exeter: The University of Exeter for the Teacher Training Agency.

Medwell, J. & Wray, D. (2007) Handwriting: what do we know and what do we need to know? *Literacy* 41, 1, pp. 10-16.

Mercer, N. & Littleton, K. (2007) *Dialogue and the Development of Children's Thinking*. London, Routledge.

Myhill, D.A., Jones, S.M., Lines, H. & Watson, A. (2012) Re-thinking grammar: the impact of embedded grammar teaching on students' writing and students' metalinguistic understanding. *Research Papers in Education* 27, 2, pp.139-166.

National Association for Language Development in the Curriculum (NALDIC) (2012) http://www.naldic.org.uk/research-and-information/eal-statistics/ealachievement Accessed 17.4.13

Neuman, S.B., And Roskos, K. (1997). Literacy knowledge in practice: contexts of participation for young readers and writers. *Reading Research Quarterly*, 32, 1, pp. 10-32.

Nixon, H. & Comber, B. (2006). Differential recognition of children's cultural practices in middle primary literacy classrooms. *Literacy*, 40, 3, pp. 127-136.

Nixon, J. & Topping, K. (2001) Emergent writing: the impact of structured peer interaction. *Educational Psychology* 21, 1, pp. 41-58.

Ofsted (Office for Standards in Education) (2011) *Excellence in English: What we can learn from 12 outstanding schools*. Manchester: Ofsted Available at: http://www.ofsted.gov.uk/resources/excellence-english Accessed 12.4.13

Opie, I. (1993) *The People in the Playground*. Oxford: Oxford University Press.

O'Sullivan, O. & Thomas, A. (2007) *Understanding Spelling*. Abingdon: Routledge.

Pantaleo, S. (2007a) The reader in the writer: exploring elementary students' metafictive texts. *The Journal of Reading, Writing and Literacy*, 2, 3, pp. 42-74.

Pantaleo, S. (2007b) Writing texts with radical change characteristics. *Literacy* 41, 1, pp. 16-25.

Parr, J. & Limbrick, L. (2010) Contextualising practice: hallmarks of effective teachers of writing. *Teaching and Teacher Education* 26, pp. 583-590.

Peters, M.L. (1970) *Success in Spelling*. Cambridge: Cambridge Institute of Education.

Pressley, M., Rankin, J. & Yokoi, L. (1996) A survey of the instructional practices of outstanding primary-level literacy teachers. *Elementary School Journal* 96, pp. 363-384.

Pressley, M., Wharton-Mcdonald, R., Allington, R., Block, C.C., Morrow, L., Tracey, D., Baker, K., Brooks, G., Cronin, J., Nelson, E. And Woo, D. (2001) A study of effective first-grade literacy instruction. *Scientific Studies of Reading* 5, 1, pp. 35-58.

Pritchard, R. J. (1987) Effects on student writing of teacher training in the National Writing Project Model. *Written Communication*, 4, 1, pp. 51-67.

Read,C. (1971) *Children's Creative Spelling*. London: Routledge & Kegan. Paul.

Riley, J. (1996). *The Teaching of Reading*. London: Paul Chapman Publishing.

Robertson, L. (2004) Multilingual flexibility and literacy learning in an Urdu community school. In E. Gregory, S. Long and D. Volk (eds.) *Many Pathways to Literacy*. London: RoutledgeFalmer.

Rowe, D. W. And Neitzel, C. (2010) Interest and agency in 2 and 3-year-olds' participation in emergent writing *Reading Research Quarterly*, 45, 2, pp.169-195.

Sipe, L. (1993) Using transformations of traditional stories: making the reading-writing connection. The Reading Teacher 47,1, pp. 18-26.

Smith, F. (1982) *Writing and the Writer*. London: Heinemann.

Snowling, M. (1994) Towards a model of spelling acquisition: the development of some component skills. In D. Gordon, A. Brown and N.C. Ellis (eds.): *The Handbook of Spelling, Theory, Process and Intervention*. Toronto: Wiley.

Solsken, J. (1993) *Literacy, Gender and Work in Families and in School*. Norwood NJ: Ablex.

Taylor, B.M., Pearson, D.P., Clark, K.F. And Walpole, S. (1999) Effective schools/accomplished teachers. *The Reading Teacher* 53, 2, pp. 156-159.

Taylor, B.M., Pearson, P.D., Clark, K. And Walpole, S. (2000) Effective schools and accomplished teachers: lessons about primary-grade reading instruction in low-income schools *The Elementary School Journal* 101, 2, 121-165.

Teale, W. H., & Gambrell, L. (2007). Raising urban students' literacy achievement by engaging in authentic, challenging work. *The Reading Teacher*, 60, 728-739.

Teale, W. & Sulzby, E. (1986) *Emergent Literacy: Writing and reading*. Norwood NJ: Ablex.

Treiman, R. (1994) Sources of information used by beginning spellers. In D. Gordon, A. Brown and N.C. Ellis (Eds): *The Handbook of Spelling, Theory, Process and Intervention*. London: Wiley.

Vivas, E. (1996) Effects of story reading on language. *Language Learning* 46:2, pp. 189-216.

Vygotsky, L. S. (1978). *Mind in Society: The development of higher psychological processes*. Cambridge, MA: Harvard University Press.

Waller, M. (2010) "It's very very fun and ecsiting" - using Twitter in the primary classroom. *English Four to Eleven* 39, pp14 -16.

Walsh, C. (2007) Creativity as capital in the literacy classroom: youth as multimodal designers *Literacy* 41 (3) 74-80.

Warrington, M., Younger, M. & Bearne E. (2006) *Raising Boys' Achievement in Primary Schools*. Buckingham: Open University Press.

Wells, G. (1985) *Language, Learning and Education*. Windsor: NFER: Nelson.

Wharton-Mcdonald, R., Pressley, M. & Hampston, J.M (1998) Literacy instruction in nine first-grade classrooms: teacher characteristics and student achievement. *Elementary School Journal* 99, 2, pp. 101-128.

Wilkinson, I. & Townsend, M. (2000) From Rata to Rimu: grouping for instruction in best practice New Zealand classrooms. *The Reading Teacher* 53, 6, pp. 460-471.

Williams, G. (1995) *Learning Systemic Functional Grammar in Primary Schools*. Macquarie: Macquarie University Style Council.

Wood, D. J., Bruner, J. S., & Ross, G. (1976). The role of tutoring in problem solving. *Journal of Child Psychiatry and Psychology* 17, 2, pp. 89-100.

Wyse, D. (1998) *Primary Writing*. Buckingham: Open University Press.

Yamada-Rice, D. (2010) Beyond Words: an enquiry into children's home visual communication practices. *Journal of Early Childhood Literacy* 10, 3, pp. 341-363

Yarrow, F. & Topping, K. (2001) Collaborative writing: the effects of metacognitive prompting and structured peer interaction. *British Journal of Educational Psychology* 71, pp. 261-282

Yeo, M. (2007) New literacies, alternative texts: teachers' conceptualisations of composition and literacy. *English Teaching: Practice and Critique* 6, 1, pp. 113-131

UKLA

Join UKLA

For more details about the United Kingdom Literacy Association visit our website at **www.ukla.org**

or write to us at

UKLA
University of Leicester
University Road
Leicester LE1 7RH

UKLA